THE BLUE HOUR

THE BLUE HOUR

CLARE CROSSMAN

All rights reserved. No part of this work covered by the copyright herein may be reproduced or used in any means – graphic, electronic, or mechanical, including copying, recording, taping, or information storage and retrieval systems – without written permission of the publisher.

Printed by imprintdigital
Upton Pyne, Exeter
www.digital.imprint.co.uk

Typesetting by narrator
www.narrator.me.uk
info@narrator.me.uk
033 022 300 39

Cover design by Víctor-Manuel Ibáñez
vm.ibanez61@gmail.com

Published by Shoestring Press
19 Devonshire Avenue, Beeston, Nottingham, NG9 1BS
(0115) 925 1827
www.shoestringpress.co.uk

First published 2017
© Copyright: Clare Crossman

The moral right of the author has been asserted.

ISBN 978-1-912524-00-6

ACKNOWLEDGEMENTS

Thanks are due to the editors of the *Interpreters House*, *Scintilla*, *Ink Sweat and Tears*, *The Poetry Shed*, *Frogmore Papers* and *More Phrog*, *The Carrot* (Cumbria), *Agenda*, *Poetry Salzburg*, *Reactions* (University of East Anglia), *London Grip*, *The Way* (Diocesan Newspaper Carlisle).

'Norwich Taxi' was written and chosen for Norwich the City of Stories and published on a beer mat for 12 weeks in that city.

'The Fire Crane' and 'The Day We went to Newcastle' are included in coming into Leaf An Anthology by Poetry ID 2015.

'The Irish Chair' first published in *Strike up the Band: Poems for John Lucas at 80* edited Merryn Williams.

'For the Woman who goes Swimming every Day' is included in *Fanfare*, editors Wendy French and Dilys Wood, *Poems by Contemporary Women Poets*.

'Crossings' included in *Other Worlds* anthology Allographic Cambridge.

'Gold Finches' was commended in Wild Life Worlds Poetry Competition Wales.

'*Fine Foods* est. 1954' is included in *Write to be Counted* Anthology, editors Nicola Jackson Jacci Bulman.

'At the Possessio of the Alfabi 23.6.16' was first published by New Boots and Pantisocraties.\Neu! August 7 2016 and is included in the Smokestack Anthology.

'The Well' was commissioned for Romsey Arts Festival 2013 by Cambridge Arts Salon.

'The Leaving' was published by Liz Cashdan for The Open College of the Arts 'Belong and Belonging' series.

'The Pear Tree' was recorded by Victor Ibanez at the Second Pivotal Festival Cambridge Introductory Reading, Winter 2016, and can be found on youtube.

'Water Light' are poems for a film with the film maker James Murray White.

I would like to thank Liz Cashdan, Kaddy Benyon, Lucy Hamilton and Lucy Sheerman (the poetry sisters) and Victor Ibanez for his cover illustration.

for Iain and in memory of Anna Crossman

Here I lie, Clock o clay
Waiting for the time of day

– John Clare, 'Clock o Clay'

A child said *What is the grass?* fetching it to me with full hands;
How could I answer the child? I do not know what it is any
    more than he

– Walt Whitman, 'A child said *What is grass?*'

CONTENTS

Norwich Taxi	1
The Blue Hour at Brown's	2
Five Portraits	3
1 The Irish Chair	3
2 Written in the Bone	4
3 Sunt lacrimae rerum	5
4 Heartsease	6
5 Ursel	7
Suddenly	8
Three Poems	9
1 The Fire Crane	9
2 The Dress	10
3 The Pear Tree	11
Coastal	12
The Summer Guest	13
Marmora Road in Summer	14
John Goode's Testament, 1510	15
The Day We went to Newcastle	17
Indelible	18
1 A 1920's Childhood	18
2 Back Fields	20
The Photographs	21
Horses in Kingsmoor Woods	22
The Boy and the Rain	23
John Bunyan of Elstow, 1628–1688	24
Life Writing	25
1 The Diary	25
2 Biographer	26

Water Light	27
1 Melbourn Bury	27
2 Falls	28
3 Mill	29
4 Map	30
5 Weir	31
6 Crossings	32
7 Vaughan Williams at Warren Bank	33
8 Waste	34
9 Confluence	35
Common Ground	36
For the Woman who goes Swimming every Day	37
Gold Finches	38
The Field	39
June at Docwra's Manor	40
The Complete Tourist	41
1 At the Possessio of Alfabi 23.6.16	41
2 Shadow Play	42
3 Stefani	43
4 Among Argentinieans	44
5 *Fine Foods* est. 1954	45
6 On Black Rock Sands	46
Gifts from Winter	47
Llanystumdwy 2017	48
The Well	49
The Leaving	50

NORWICH TAXI

'This city has a signature', she said,
driving the taxi up the Unthank Road.
'A fortress for the territory,
it writes in spires, cobble stones,
scores circles of tree-shaded streets.
I came home for sun on buildings,
history in walls. It is its own destination.

Beyond is nowhere but weather,
where else could you go but the sea?'

THE BLUE HOUR AT BROWN'S

Ice clinks in a bucket and a woman
in a fur coat runs to kiss a man
wearing a grey suit. Already
girls on skyscraper heels, and clouded
in Chanel are ordering champagne.
It is the hour of coming in,
the afternoon has dissolved
into dark.

The revolving door propels
others inwards from the street.
Meetings reflected in the mirror
behind the burnished bar. 'And then'
John said, 'I liked making people
cry, so I was furious with him.
Anyway it's over'—her mobile blinks
away another life.

I will never know, beginning, middle,
end. What happens to the boy
who leans to touch his girlfriend's face.
The blue hour, loved by film makers:
where day becomes dusk,
night descending in low light
from the lamps and polite waiters
polishing glasses, pretending not to listen.
So I invent this winter intimacy,
an old romance, where outside
it is cold enough for snow.

FIVE PORTRAITS

1 The Irish Chair

> 'Say not the struggle, nought availeth' – Arthur Hugh Clough

My mother is the one who haunts me most
and often sits in the wooden Irish chair.
Putting on a coat I think of her, the way she said
'This will see me out.' I understand that now,
the decades running low. And how she was
angry when she said she'd lost her dinner
and when I laughed said 'It isn't funny growing old.'

And then there was her word when she despaired
at people's demands, their shabby behaviour.
'When all else fails, *imagine*.'
Or of a novel she enjoyed 'I think that this
Is seriously good. I'm not lending it to you
If you keep it in a maw!'

Fierce blue eyes, white hair, she'd melt
like snow. Close all the curtains
in the house even in the summer dusk.
'There's so much terrible suffering in
the world. Let's shut it out.'

During winter we would light the fire,
turn the television on, sit in our ancient jumpers
drinking whisky to keep warm.
In the large granite house, surrounded by a field,
miles from nowhere, quite often she'd remark:
'I could quite easily live on buns.'

2 Written in the Bone

Why do I mind so much when
my neighbour, John is away?
Is it because I know that he is not
there to check accounts or do the parish books,
or be found digging on his allotment?

I don't bump into him walking through the wood,
his blue cotton cap and long white hair
suggesting, in another age, they might
have called him prophet.
Given that he is often hefting branches,
cutting logs and wondering
what will happen to the green.

His car has been parked up for 27 days
and the back garden has gone completely wild,
sending messages of feral seeds
beyond hedges and into the street,
to any pavement that will hold them.

I tell myself it is because he cares.
Looks across the boundaries,
takes time to consider his part of the town.
In case you think he's gone away
to take part in circle dancing; he is
travelling along the Eastern desert roads
to understand what is tribal,
or what perhaps is written in the bone.

3 Sunt lacrimae rerum

Miss Winnerah is a Roman was compassed
into my desk. How many years it had been
there on the lid, I don't know.
She taught Latin, chiselled face, marbled hair,
smelled of chalk, seemed part of
the classical world she lectured us about:
the Acropolis and the broken-handed gods.

Someone had drawn her as a statue.
Beside the deputy headmistress scratched
as a stick, they blew words at each other
in cartoon bubbles *'Silence Please'*
and *'sunt lacrimae rerum.'* Miss Bland,
sleeves of her graduation gown hanging
like a bat, often screeched at us.

Away from what seemed wrinkled,
dusted, we took to walking
by the river, beside brown water
that rushed through the rocks
and garlic flowers. Shiny and new,
long limbed and seventeen, that was
the only place to take our philosophies.

Hidden among trees, never caught,
laughing and smoking,
where else could we go
except into that green?
Not knowing then that
there are tears for things.

"There are tears at the heart of things" – *Virgil Book 1 line 462 Aeneid*, trans. Seamus Heaney

4 Heartsease

(For Dan, 1927–2015)

You have had enough of us and our demands.
We talk when you want to sleep,
take you shopping when you'd rather read.
In this small flat, its television and bowl of soup
for one; your wife and friends, gone missing.
In the hospice, they have let in air,
given company and order,
your head on pillows, supported.

Outside the window, there's a pond.
Cowslips and primroses edge the grass
as in the fields you tended,
on the market garden:
tomatoes and lettuces under
greenhouse glass, turned a penny,
put food on the table.

That was your life when peace came.
A rhythm of years, somewhere to live,
neighbours who called by to 'blether',
when your children had sailed away,
downstream.
You slept this afternoon and were
suddenly gone. No longer the difficulty
of remembering our names.
Wherever you are I wish you heartsease,
blossom on a row of cherry trees
like those outside your house.
The wild fell places, where bee orchids grow.

5 Ursel

Even in hot weather she wears a tied-on hat.
Cotton, gathered around her head,
as if she was a Black Forest shepherdess
come down from the mountain.
In her soft German accent she says

'I'm from the East you know,
for a long time I could not go back'.

She makes me think of gingerbread and pine trees,
a musk of folk tales from beside the long sweep
of the Mosel we visited as children, in a country
of courtesy, courtyards and clocks.
She tells me about her father, lost in a distant
desert campaign, buried in an unmarked grave.

'At 17 I stood at the Hamburg Harbour's edge,
as if I balanced planets on my shoulders.'

My friend, at 78, carries her own map
and avoids walls. New world in front,
old behind. She walks everywhere,
speaks three languages, a constant traveller,
translating this to that, that to this.

SUDDENLY

(For Anna)

Owls have come to sit in our fir trees:
they don't often leave the wood by the river,
I dislike their return.

I have seen their wings as they drop,
catching mice on the bright fell,
carrying them skyward, screeching.

Like omens, they have arrived
just as you are suddenly gone.
Dark eyed and serious, twenty and dead.

What you were, who you might be
snuffed out to be owl-pellets
strewn on the lawn.

I can't ask you what it is like to be fixed
in one time and place; this date in mid-summer.
Vanished, to be perpetually a bright shooting star.

Become a girl who hunts across heaven,
with a golden bow and arrow,
and comets for a crown.

Enough to say we are dumb.
Hooting one note like these birds
with the wing-span of angels.

Older. Diminished.
We blink in the July dark.
Unable to conjure you home.

THREE POEMS

> "It is good, at certain hours of the day and night, to look closely at the world of objects at rest. From them flow the contacts of man with the earth, like a text for troubled lyricists."
> – Pablo Neruda, *Towards an Impure Poetry*

1 The Fire Crane

Bitter February mornings are the music
it plays. Old tune of coal burner,
and grate, firing the coke, sharp noise
of clinker drop. Clunk of oven door.

Turning out ash, salvaged in a carrying pan,
to be earth marker on the path
covering slippery snow.

Watchman of burning, bakers and steel men,
coal bucket, hod and shiver,
chestnuts and potatoes.
Blunt instrument—it could kill a man,
but it remains, keeper of flame, gloves
and reddened faces, steak pie, warmth
for backs after long mornings working
in the fields.

The heavy moulded hand, two fingered,
keeps burning at bay.
Creak and clank of iron joints,
opening a hot door, closing the furnace
of the bellowing stove.
Sounding a riddle, where snow crystals
shatter and the dark turns back:
utensil, ordinary, of use.

2 The Dress

The yellow silk dress, hand printed with
black feathers, stitched label from
a dress shop in Chelsea, has been
in my wardrobe, all the years I moved
across counties.

Late forties chic, I could sell it as vintage
but I can't give away: the tiny cap sleeves
to enhance arms that shimmer and reach,
waist for a girl so thin she would
blow away in the slightest wind.

For me it's the click of her shoes
as she leaves the family house, pearls
at her neck, lime tree growing up through
the pavement, to go through the city
and meet him the day they get engaged.

Twenty one, in that time, after the war
which when she looked back
she remembered as polite and kind.

The skirt folds a quiet of white table cloths,
spread for afternoon tea, an old perfume
of the time they spent talking about
the weeds in the bombed-out houses,
how they would tailor the years ahead.

Unborn, I am there with them then:
wine in a glass, their books folded down,
sitting together, after a day at the races.
My mother in the dress, my father
in a neat demob suit, young and beginning.

3 The Pear Tree

Cut down to make room for a car,
for thirty years it signalled spring,
ancient and blossomed, one solitary
pear tree on the 1970's estate.
Semaphore of beginnings, outrider
of the greenwood, first headiness of summer,
it filled my head with light
each time I passed.

Flowers whiter than plaster walls,
dark juices and roots put down to earth.
From rain-spattered bark,
a shimmer of fruit falling
on the pavement in October,
available to anyone who passed.

So I put it here, to raise my voice
for the transience of weather.
For Golden Spice, Waterville,
Sauvignac, and Flemish Beauty,
pear teas, petals and enchantment.
The cooks who came for windfalls,
the juice-glutted wasps,
the branches in orchards that
shaded doorways with thin sun,
self-seeding and all ragged things.
For what we do not own,
and may never know.

COASTAL

You and I in the rattling house
set far out at the edge of fields
marking the end of the narrow road.

The touchstone of the latch
opens onto the long dune grass
and empty yellow sand.

Two miles to walk to the nearest shop
along a beach path, we find what the sea
has left green rope, broken boxes,

perfect eye socket
in the bone head of a bird.
In the petrol chugging of a lobster boat

the fall of a rock is a shout,
the shingle sifts
in the tide.

The water brings to the door
what it found on other shores,
flotsam of washed out plastic,

bottles written in different languages
that float like anemones
abandoned in brown crab pools.

Wind burns the edge of morning.
No longer landlocked, we are back
in the place we came from.

Flare from a flint, the sky endless.
We hear our breath in the salted light,
an ancient shanty of sea and air.

THE SUMMER GUEST

After an old friend has gone there is an ache.
The rooms seem emptier than before.
We begin from the last time we met,
suddenly our daughters are the age we think
we are and we can't go back to
when decades were easy to ignore.

There is no need to explain.
We travelled paths we partly chose.
Our history balances and rests.

At the farm shop where I go to buy
apples a small boy is crying.
His father comforts him: 'It's
alright to be sad when your friends
have gone'.

She has left her small coffee cup,
put down in conversation
beside the chair.
She will be back—
the day falls then rises like a wave.

MARMORA ROAD IN SUMMER

Blink and you miss it: this city garden
that grows in a space on what was
rubble and waste ground.
A circular path defines a patch of grass.
Custodian of mint, rosemary and sage,
loved with French marigolds and daisies,
a sycamore and pear tree stake out the edge.
A notice, written in hand, reads:
'A garden of earthly delights'.

Dug back from concrete, the earth breaks
through in vegetable beds: beans, lettuces,
cornflowers. One bench
and dust for sparrows,
a place to live outside, to name a flower,
breathe-in light evenings.

Born out of the refuge of blossom,
harvested for sunlight and picnics.
Faces on the surface of the water butt,
reflect, then disappear.
Made of air and weather,
as the dog rose is.

JOHN GOODE'S TESTAMENT, 1510

(after the Churchwardens' Book of Bassingbourn,
Cambridgeshire).

John Eyeworth and I paid 2d for the book
and 3d for a minstrel: his voice and his songs.
Thomas said it was too expensive but his lute
was without strings, due to fight over sheep.
We rode, two days to Bury,
the great cathedral,
to hire our play of St George:
martyr, soldier and saint.

Work and gifts were donated for the making
of swords, £3.19 was not enough for
the handles, their delicate tracery.
The dragon made of sailcloth came
in a cart, it needed repainting. Too long
in the vaults under the towers of university
holy men, had dampened its roar.

We argued over who should play the King.
Some favoured a soldier back from the Crusades.
But one leg was missing and his eye was lost
and Widow Linton's son was golden haired,
handsome, and she related to a Lord.
There was nearly a riot, but it was July,
the weather full of swifts. Priests
filled the air with blessings.

We came in procession, argumentative, blunt.
Hollow drum and flute, out of tune,
garment maker, children, all shapes of men,
following the pageant cart that turned
the Hell Wheel. For this was England 1510.
And I was John Goode,

Keeper of Parish books,
craftsman, mender, making do.

Moses fell off a cart into a midden,
Joan gave birth in a field. Richard went home
garlanded with girls. All went unpaid.
1,000 pints of ale were drunk.
There was a fire in the ricks.
Some came barefoot,
it took many years to regrow the corn.

THE DAY WE WENT TO NEWCASTLE

(i.m. AW)

Tidying out the garden shed I found them,
the bamboo shelves, covered in cobwebs,
survived fifteen winters,
still folded into three neat rows.

We carried our purchases back
on the bus that day from the northern
Chinatown. Escaped from the countryside,
to the city, for alleyways, exciting as souks,
having set out to find an Indian cotton dress,
for you to dance in.
So your arms could stretch, your feet
step freely across the floor.

It is odd to see how strong the shelves are.
Our heads full of sky, evenings spent laughing,
I didn't understand then that you were frail.
To you, the only thing that mattered was
a choreography only you could describe.

Lost to you now, the day we went to Newcastle
and carried the folded shapes of our continents home.
Which was our journey east, walls giving way to
stone Northumbrian towns
and wind from the sea.

Two bedouins crossing country,
reaching for the places between us,
we could never quite touch.

INDELIBLE

(For my father)

1 A 1920's Childhood

(The Granby Hotel, Harrogate.)

Outside the windows of the long hotel,
there are men and women queuing in the rain.
It does not seem like this when you run
along the corridor toward the kitchen
where the cook is making toast.
Your morning smells of breakfast.

From the back there's a view of allotments.
People dig all day and pick the sky high beans,
wrap them in newspaper, whistling.

You are told there has been a war.
Old men with broken faces covered
in tin masks are selling matches.
Your mother plays the piano every day
because your father came home.

Luck has brought you here.
Your grandfather's ball-bearing eyes,
his aptitude for maths, his guesses
at the main chance.
You help fold the large white sheets.

The French governess, 'Madame'
comes every week. Her heels clack.
You must learn the language of travel,
French names for wine, the words waiters speak.

You hang up damp overcoats
of strangers who arrive in the rain,
are allowed to dress up as a chef
to serve stern men their dinners,
as in the silent films you go to with your brother.

You have a daily matinee,
are running down a modern tunnel
to where the European cities wait.
When you reach the light,
you will translate, another dark.

2 Back Fields

Not much, but it was where we crossed between
the houses. One gravel path over a scrubland
of grass where most hurried to town
and no one minded about the dogs.

We got to know the small on tin trays.
Makeshift toboggans, flying toward
the eel sheds and factories beside the sludge-filled
River Medway, with its iron bridge to Strood.

Face down we'd press our hands into the snow
until we saw the grass, hidden and wet,
like summer which seemed years away.
I fell and grazed my knees, stung clean with iodine.

We were shown how dandelions blow clocks
and daisies make a chain. I never learned to
sound a grass note from the single spike
threaded through my hands, but learned seasons,

the shape of ground under my feet, that
not everything is written by us. I could
not read the heavy memorial plaque riveted
to the entrance wall: *'Donated 1918*

in memory of a fallen son.' Unbuilt on,
Backfields still hurtles children under the sky,
history held forever in the grey stone walls
that witness those who lived to walk the river.

THE PHOTOGRAPHS

Here are some that I never took:
the view from upstairs across to the town
that lit up like a fairground in winter.
The green swell of fields,
the swoop and delight of swallows returning.
One light in a window beyond the dark trees.
Hard to catch the first breath of frost,
the musk scent of stubble, shape of dog rose
hedgerows in summer.

Those years will never form lines
or follow each other in easy succession,
profusion not belonging in one dimension.
But each time I make the journey north
it is to those rooms I am going back.
The grey house on the rise that withstood
the weather. Pressed into memory
like a petal smudged on window glass,
wind under the door in winter,
lanes rutted to iron hard.

Will they see me when I return?
A step on the stair, a glimpse
of a face, a bare arm, hem, a shadow
they can't shake, a line of colour,
passe-partout?

HORSES IN KINGSMOOR WOODS

'The swiftes horse, these bells to tak for mi lade Daker sake'.
– Prize at Carlisle Horse Races, 1580

Their presence still in the trees, ash,
alder and oak where the wood has grown up
over the moor where they raced for the prize of a bell.

Black ponds are dark eyes in the new green
of the cow parsley riot. Mist rising like breath or
steam from flanks. Puddles, stamped hoof marks

in the bluebell shock, along cinder paths
wide enough to canter. Out of shadow and weather,
tree branches shape them in grassed glades.

Where fast trains flash past the old sidings,
hidden here in the green woods and summer rain,
at the edge, a rumour of horses, a tenderness gained.

Part of the mud, grey mare and stallion,
snatching grass, billowing lips, whisk of a mane.
As if they might appear among the warehouse containers,

the stickle-back ditch, the yards of new houses.
They ring in the rustle where branches drip,
an otherworld lightness that cannot be tamed.

THE BOY AND THE RAIN

He keeps the car window open to feel
it on his face. Listens for drumming
on dustbins, tin roofs, the pavement.
A closure and an ending to an afternoon
of heat or those winter nights
when all the windows in the street
are blurred to Christmas decorations.

He has come to know the rain.
Each splash a taste of sea inland.
Where rain begins and ends is in clouds,
the unknowable distance between thermals.
He joins those who dance in it,
water on their skin,
knowing it's their natural element.

There's wildness in its fall, a solace
of uneasy corners, wet flapping edges.
Unpredictable, it comforts. Puts an end
to crying, washes the street clean,
melts what was high definition to
somewhere else that is inward,
a clean silver ribbon of road,
a new beginning of sorts.

JOHN BUNYAN OF ELSTOW, 1628–1688

Returned, a soldier, from the war with the King,
one of Cromwell's men, another man
took a shot meant for him.

So it was grace he believed that brought him home
to the bowl of the Bedfordshire sky. To hear women
on their front steps talking of a plain God.

In the rough hillocks of heavy clay John Bunyan
of Elstow by the ancient Ouse River
heard epistles drawn on the air.

His work, pen and ink, a black scatter of writing
like footsteps on a white sermon's pages.
A rising of spirit, the outspoken let free.

Then far from speaking, silenced for his views
 in prison he was a tinker again. Always a pilgrim,
not far from the roads, making laces for shoes.

From the hinterlands quietly, a faith
necessary as water and bread. Out of the middle,
 and in-between, The Straight Gate,

the Slough of Despond, All stations on the way
to the Delectable Mountains that are heaven,
further and higher than we can ever be.

LIFE WRITING

1 The Diary

I have been with them all day
in the house they shared.
Red sandstone walls holding
the shadow of branched apple trees
and the plain deep Cumbria hearth.
They read novels aloud most evenings,
made hay in high summer,
from the garden grass.

And I following each day now,
revisit their lives,
where sun still falls across the paper.
Walk with them along the river,
spend afternoons on the tideless marsh
as they watched their footprints fade.

Outside the window, the moon floats
in bitter wood-smoke frost.
I feel the summer green,
the grain of them, again.

There are drawings of each new season.
She describes her need for silence
'Then the winter came
turning everything to snow.'

A decade gone. I turn on the lamp
and we are together again in the same room.
But these pages are, all ink and rustle,
shadows folded, like the feathers
of a white birds wing. A careful manuscript
of what happened a long time ago.

2 Biographer

No one will ever know
what happened to the green scarf
you wore, the long winter skirts

given away in a different city
for someone else to wear.
At the Indian table others

will be drinking tea, no sense
that you were there. If there
is a ghost, I haven't seen one

except sometimes there is a likeness
when someone tall and elegant walks
toward me.

Or if I stand close to the chestnut tree
where you are scattered, it seems
you are mapped into the wind.

Diaries not in sequence and gaps of years,
underneath the ink I can still hear you
speak to me.

'These things we kept for our records', they said.
Certificates of competence in History and French,
a family tree tracing a lost connection.

But I can no longer ask what happened
in-between. Was it you who painted
the primroses in the wood?

I close the box file, thinking how your handwriting
changed as you grew older, and in the kitchen
I still have the old cup you drank your coffee from.

WATER LIGHT

"The way is broad, reaching left as well as right."
– Lao Tzu, *Tao Te Ching Book One XXXIV*

(The River Mel is a chalk stream which rises in Melbourn, Cambridgeshire, and joins the Cam at Malton Lane, Malton, after eight miles.)

1 Melbourn Bury

At the rising place, a bare lake
come from aquifer, deep spring,
an accident of geology.
Clear as an eye,
straight from the source,
chalk water spilling through my hands.

The Anglo Saxons left their cups,
the sharp edges of their brooches here.
Votive, for protecting
a washing, drinking place.

If this river has a god it's Hestia.
Goddess of settlement and hearth.
After the silver jewels fall,
here is a house, path, bridge
and a name: Bury: meaning
secret, hidden, enfolded
underground.

2 Falls

The lake becomes a thin stream.
Falls on its own current to a narrow trace.
Written in shallows, gravel bed and ankle high,
a narrative of greengage orchards and plums.
A summer to spend wading on the clay bottom.
Here be dragon flies, cool places where
reed beds clump.
If this chalk stream were more than element
it would know that in this curving fall
 it carries memory, losses, griefs
away across this meadow
and that here we live by waterlight.

3 Mill

Posing in a tiny photograph
with their crooked grins,
at the iron bridge
this is where the whippet boys swam

into the weeds for treasure.
Alongside the rat and the watervole,
at the place of the sharp divers,
pearly white kings of the water.

But a long wire from farm fencing
trapped a boy's ankle
and he did not rise.
The water plastered over his head.

Now the pond smiles with waterlilies,
old millstones as ornament
and souvenir, beyond its dark history.
A black depth held back,

where it sloshes for release
behind the rusted sluice gate.
Waiting.

4 Map

Shapeshifting and marking time,
too narrow for boats,
the stream cuts through playing fields,
connecting villages to woods,
the footpaths pounded for walks,
outward and home.

It collects rain,
has its own damp and dog hole
that fills with plastic bottles crisp packets,
thrown from passing cars.
The stream carries the reflections
of the backs of houses,
watering fields and giving places
to rest your mind on water.

In summer it reclaims green.
Water parsnip, long rustling reeds
willow trees shimmer.
Keeps winter in its sump,
rivery mist rising on iced mornings.

Mostly it contains the sky.
A field of blue or iron grey,
etched with trees.
Never the same.
This silver thread
that ties places together
with a mirror. And every day,
a new rite of passage.

5 Weir

The rush that turned the mill wheel
is a waterfall now,
its gush and race funnels like a great rain
that fills a hollow deep enough to swim in.

On June days swifts dive
between the two large stones
that hold the empty shaft of its tunnel.

Here the stream is gathered in,
in the water dark below the grain tower
it lets go of the weight it carries,
releases its possibilities into
the widening calm of gravel shallows,
water light flickering copper in the sun.

Leaning over at the small bridge
to watch things pass:
The birds skim back into the air.
The daylight floats.
The collected branches,
broken wood, decaying leaves
these too are washed away.

6 Crossings

The chalk stream claims its territory
in a scrap book of feathers,
watermarked weeds, pressed petals,
insect wings.

No fords, only tiny stone bridges
or firm wooden crossings that would take a horse,
a flock of sheep, as was once.

Behind the church there's willow shelter
on the banks, picture perfect. Sanctuary
as if it were still an ancient way
full of travelling ghosts.

One minute, long grass, the next chalk flat.
And it is as if nothing ever changes
and crossing is easy between banks.
Through the gate, forward and back
forward and back.

But this is the nature
of crossings, a leaving, a letting go
a threshold.

There were others here before.

7 Vaughan Williams at Warren Bank

He felt the music rising in his head,
then in flat land wind under a ringing sky.

And walked out from the gloomy house
to travel white dust roads to find the singing.

From the field men of work sitting with their ale
waiting to tell stories and the women

with lullabies and broken hearted girls
laments twisted from the briars of love.

He set them down turned into plain song,
to become natural as the grieving river,

unstopping as the water that connects
source, millpond and moving shallows,

to be part of the stave, the largo and heft
of the quietly beating heart.

8 Waste

This man is made of water
as the girl was made of flowers.
Riffle and shift, rain collects.
He knows the stream from its scent,
silt and knotweed,
hawthorn buds, the green
prophecy of spring.

Crossing his land, the river
is a ditch, full of plastic cartons.
Deep steep banks, shelving
so it can't rise and is beyond the wind.
Once he found a message in a bottle
jammed in the drain.
'Come back' it said.

All his family washed in it,
his sons looked for trout
some grew watercress,
he does not want it rising
to a flood.

The man is made of water
as the girl was made of flowers.
Riffle and shift it crosses his land.
In dry weather he uses it
for storage, when the ditch fills with dust.

9 Confluence

And suddenly there is a wider river,
approaching across the plain
like the Amazon passing through.
Risen from a thousand wells,
it cannot stop flowing seaward.

The thin chalk stream joins it.
Trickles in willowed enchantment: flag iris,
rosebay willow herb, cool
clay bed at the place where fish
might swim upstream.

Confluence. Noun. A flowing together
of two or more streams.
A body of water formed by two
Rivers or lakes. It happens here
on land miles from nowhere
at a boundary and a border.

Water finds water unless it's dammed.

COMMON GROUND

Anecdote of a route, it curves across country,
a well trodden song line: chalk track, footpath,
right of way, wide enough for horses
and barking dogs. Pulling you into fields
through the long grass; green and damp with rain.

An old current of walking-out-with,
way-to-work, chance meetings and conversations
between villages, opening to new places.
History embedded in the ground below your feet.

Corner, twist and turn, how to get there told
by word of mouth and trespass. A map of
landmark trees and flowers with folk names:
Herb Robert, Jack by the Hedge,
Eyebright, Ladies' Smock.

On this walk to the river with only the sky
to notice you as you pass, the wood gives
up its songs: of larks rising, grey lag geese
honking a B minor note, a sudden hare,
blackberries before the curse of winter frost.

May the wide stubble fields that stretch
beyond the eye to the land's edge
not be a language lost to us. As the crab apple
blossoms, as the stile opens, as the crow flies,
as the weather turns, as the sun goes in
when the moon rises.

FOR THE WOMAN WHO GOES SWIMMING EVERY DAY

No longer of earth, she is liquid now:
the water around her frees her to float.
As long as she's in that air gone element,
she is buoyant as clouds, acrobatic:
a trapeze artist dancing the high wire.

All embracing, it holds her, there is no one
to say what shape she should make.
Small children are fishes, their mothers
anemone shoals loosed from rock pools.
Arms and legs are white underwater
like porcelain or a new born's skin.

She can be who she wishes:
queen of the depths, not of the ground.
All gestures are hers, she has a view to
the bottom and top. Who says she is not
a siren of the deep?
All breath and sinew,
words float away to reflections.

With each stroke she pushes back
against all that is dark, swimming lengths,
catching sun, making her own choreography,
an original dance,

become a girl in the first month of summer,
at the first place of knowing,
in the silence, restored.

GOLD FINCHES

They came, a pair of them, red balaclavas,
burning their shapes on the morning.
Bright yellow flashes on black speckled wings.

They balanced each side of the foxglove stalk.
Winter seeds the best, matured,
encased; preserved from frost.

Each wing, each bird foot,
perfectly balanced. Every hovering
gesture, a gold finch pas de deux.

I'd never seen them so closely before
pure double act; lead and fall guy like
a couple of costumed spivs.

Working stealthily, confiscating coins,
up to the mark, dressed in their best,
two flamboyant masked raiders.

They couldn't see me behind
the bedroom window. My view better
than television, better than any hide.

As if a veil had opened onto, fearless
and undaunted. Then a goods train rattled past,
and they vamoosed like highwaymen,

back to where no one could ever tame them.

THE FIELD

The field has never been cut.
He drives past it every day,
waits for those afternoons in June
when it is full of fritillary, eyebright,
bugle and buttercups.
Flowers that have seeded themselves,
blown in from the road.
He thinks he should keep a diary,
become an amateur naturalist,
note the date of the first star flower,
and when the rosebay signals that
the year is turning to dewed webs in the grass.
Privately he calls it the burning field.
It seems to flicker every golden colour
and he could paint it from memory.
He trespasses with his children regularly.
Emerging from the wood at the bottom
they lie down among the couch grass heads
that point to heaven and wait to
feel the earth turning.
In buildings and cities,
he returns to the endless blue,
they've seen above their heads
the way the field waits under snow
and then suddenly is full of ladybirds and green.
The field stays with him,
a wild meadow, always returning summer,
where his daughter chases butterflies
and grass seed drops in sandwiches,
and he lies head to head with his son,
pretending to be Indians.
He thinks that Paradise may be like that.

JUNE AT DOCWRA'S MANOR

The courtyard is a snatch of a far country.
The paving stones absorb heat from the sun,
water lilts of the sea and a quenched thirst.

Here is for fig and lavender to grow.
And rosemary its rust taste, strong as honey.
There might be lemons or a jasmine covered wall.

Enclosed, we sit here in summer pretending
we are high in the mountains, tin bells of goats
at the edge of hearing, in the clear air.

The lily pollen on my hands soaks a rain charm.
Slowly the grasses dry and the heads of artichokes
burn among the green.

Swallows arrive with high calls and indigo wings.
In their returning they dart between doors,
sit high in the eaves, studding the day.
This is one way to bring the distance home.

I sit on this terrace, half awake, sun behind my eyes.
In the daylight's unravelling,

what language should I speak?

THE COMPLETE TOURIST

1 At the Possessio of Alfabi 23.6.16

A wooden Flemish chair carved with
the myth of Tristran and Isolde,
under a bright wooden Mudejar ceiling,
 inscribed with words from the Koran.
And beyond an open gate, the courtyard
and the road, with stone benches to sit on
under the cypress trees' deep shade.

In the elegance of this Spanish farmhouse:
a cellar with an olive press and stables,
and above rooms with windows open
to the mountains and the Moorish garden,
with palms and irrigation channels
spreading water to the sun.
The swallows dive and Chopin is
being played on the terrace.

I note a filigree of shadow in the
olive branches on the hot path.
Not of me anymore. My country
is reflected in the amazement
of the Spanish gardener's eyes.
His shrug at a pasty-faced people
who want lawns and cathedrals
and pretty flowers in their private gardens.
Which have no strangeness to them,
and are white, completely white.

Possessio = Mallorcan/Spanish for farm estate.

2 Shadow Play

Leaving Ibiza town, driving along
the rocky coast, I remembered you:
the cove we camped in with your son
under the southern stars, the nights lit
by fires, lanterns, and open doors.
And the bars where we drank coffee,
where long legged women walked barefoot
under the rattan, flicking back their hair
and talking about life in the mountains.

We didn't reach those adobe places
high up in the pines with hot
afternoons to lie together sleeping.
Our moons were sugar-paper thin,
made of white sand, a myth of tides,
salt spray in our faces when we sailed
between the islands.

Like the papier maché dragon;
you gave me as a gift, bought from
the Balinese back lit shadow play we saw
breathing smoke as it danced,
all drumming and reversals,
then disappearing, invisible
behind the screen.

Much as a the sea boom at midnight
defies the quiet of an evening wind,
or Mediterranean water turns to ink
breaking heavy waves across starlight.
Much as the bright ephemera of awnings,
the shadows on this bleached road,
remind me of that time; the puppet play
and the fire that burned dark.

3 Stefani*

This May I am returning home to my village,
away from the petrol and dust of the city.
Born from rain and the January dark,
the wildflowers seem to grow out
of air: chamomile, iris, oregano, daisies.
As if Zeus had scattered them all
as he passed. I will braid them to circle,
hang them at my door. Bind a sheaf
with an ear of wheat for Demeter.

We were always sailors, fish of the river,
voyaging out from green waters
into the Aegean, or traders searching
for ivory, obsidian, amber and glass.
When invaders came we had the mountains,
partisan, bare. Or we lived in
the forests, waited high up with the goats.

The world is an eye that can turn blue.
I prefer a white horse, this yard full of shade,
time to sit at the table with friends.
The sea at my door.
There are too many islands to take.
While I am here it is right I think
to believe in light and flowers.

*Greek Spring Festival, May 1st

4 Among Argentinieans

From the dust of Buenos Aires they have
come from the white clay houses
and grand squares, dressed in their best:
gold bracelets, neatly tailored suits for Consuelo's exhibition.

The caravan is propped in an English field,
May buttercups, sheep in the distance.
The paintings spill and dazzle, red, black
and orange, a small piece of South America.

In the absence of palm trees, we eat olives
and sweet cakes, as she explains: 'I painted
this woman embracing the sun. She is
a jewelled butterfly, so I edged her wings with lace.'

The hot afternoon is conquistador at the door.
Outside the studded interior shade. At each
new arrival the cry is 'ola'. Struggling with
the phrases I lean back into cool in courtyards

where shutters keep us hidden. 'This woman is free
to go anywhere born from a chrysalis,
she can leave home behind'. The pictures
dazzle and defy, the light they hold glares.

Before we leave she makes black coffee,
the row of rooks on the trees blaze.
Her gold cross glints. Only later does she
speak of the generals who made them migrant.

5 *Fine Foods* est. 1954

I remember Mr Perowicz's shadowed
delicatessen, the sausages wrapped in paper
and cut by hand.
Tomatoes, onions, gherkins
in vinegar, as if summer was kept in jars.
He'd put the shelves in necessary order.

Neat in his white overall, he kept his counsel
and never said how he'd arrived
or why he'd fled.
It was personal to him, his walk
to work through our provincial town-
a freedom, or a journey of forgetting.

It was his wife who negotiated
belonging. In sentences of night class
grammar, she spoke when she took
the money. I stuttered 'schleb'
when I asked for bread.

I loved the cool difference of their shop,
the smells of cabbage and cheese,
as if it was a slice of earth.
A gate to lean on in their country,
the names in unpronounceable script,
a somewhere else of marbled surfaces,
light held immaculate in glass.

That was our exchange,
what they had always known
and what was new to me; an exile
made of Pomeranian salt, amber,
and herring-silver. Another place
rich and harsh, as the slate grey
distance from the Baltic sea.

6 On Black Rock Sands

The child at the edge is making her own world,
scouting rock pools, picking up shells,
retracing her footprints, forward and back.

It seems there are light years between
mother and her: they can't agree.
The shoreline echoes with shouts.

Faraway she is walking the strand,
taking chances, pretending:
a shrugged silhouette in the distance.

Favoured, her brother and sister sit on
the hot sand, neatly below the grassed dunes.
Standing apart in the overcast day,

she has the sea where nothing is fixed:
it can change in a second, on the tilt of a seabird's
wing. The invisible stars are passing.

The tide rolls in above the crabs and anemones.
Pools become sky, in the bay there are boats,
the waves and the water dissolve her shadow.

GIFTS FROM WINTER

Here's dogwood for its everlasting colour, seed heads
and hawthorn berries once used for decorating cakes.

Here's chocolate, orange, and honey, preserving
green leaves and bees, the touch of summer on your tongue.

Here's a lighted room, wine and soup,
the dark closed out, an evening in with friends.

Here's the first white scape of snow and a bare
Tree the wind has bent back in a fence of frost.

Here's slush and footsteps, boots,
and fireside reading.

Here's memory, sleep, and returning home
on journeys in the dark of badly-lit closed towns.

Here's wool and tweed, vests, socks,
knitted hats, slowly adding another skin.

Here's a red velvet rose, sewn from summer.
Nothing can steal its glamour, the moment it describes.

Here's crazy fire, its heat and light that burns,
Sky lantern, torch, lamps to defy the night.

Here are the stars in a remembered place
where frost is feathers, water, glass.

Here's the world for one day silver, lit by love.
If we can still believe that story told long ago,

that innocence came on a December night,
despite the iron of snow.

LLANYSTUMDWY 2017

> 'From there you will be able to get
> down to the sea.' – Liz

Sand from between the new green hedges
on the hawthorn path falls grainy and gritty
out of my shoes, unworldly, shifting.

In this place where land slips to salted distance,
so wide your mind rests on horizons
and forgets everything, except the fishing boat's trail.

At the seaweed creek, stamped with mussel brine,
a man has made a tower of current washed pebbles.
He is lying next to it, staring at the sun.

On a day in which you have dressed, washed
gone down to the shore to listen to the water
see it spun blue in the coastal light.

Arriving home, the tide turning
won't leave my mind.
No rain, just the cove sheltering, curved,

the sea scattering brittle shells and a sky, writing.

THE WELL

(for Cambridge Art Salon)

Extending the house, they discovered a well:

a perfect brick circle, stopped with a stone.
Buttoned up against winter, the street,
hidden from spring; eye closed, keeping
its depth, sleeping in midnight
outside the weather.

An old plumb line to the place of the bucket,
jostle and voices at the horses' return.
A splash and a sweep across the hot yard,
thump of sheets on the ground, between
conversations. Water, poured,
carried for mercy to the houses of the dead.
For the threshing of grain and a loaf of bread,
bottles of beer, sold in shops
and pubs, in the drove of the day.

They opened it up: to drop pennies
and wonder at what lives in the depths,
swims at the bottom.
Meeting point, solace, dust washed
from spices, flaring a small brooch of stars.
For a tin cup of water quenching thirst
in hot summer, placating the length
of a dog's tongue.

A necessary place to sit down,
like an old song remembered,
surfaces revealed catching light
and the dance of what is.

THE LEAVING

In case we never return,
I am taking a jar of rain.

Bottled at source from butts
and puddles in early May.
Something green: seeds of mustard
and cress, moss-coloured wool,
a piece of copper for imprinting
verdigris on every surface.

The jar will lie in the cool
closed suitcase and if I
forget, I'll hold the glass
to my face,
let the liquid slosh its
messages of storms-

heedless blackthorn blossom,
blast of air on corners.
The taste of leaves and streams
on a warm April day inscribed with sun,
after the last cold nights of spring.
An atomiser of weather,

for another country:

where I walk two worlds,
migrant, as others, carrying home.